Can you do this?

I can dig

by Jenny Taylor
and Terry Ingleby

"I can dig,"
said the man.

"I can dig,"
said the dog.

"I can dig,"
said the badger.

"I can dig,"
said the woman.

"I can dig,"
said the steam shovel.

"I can dig,"
said the rabbit.

"Yes,"
said the girl.
"I can dig, too."

Which of these can dig?

fly

girl

badger

woman